Dante and Beatrice

BY
SARA KING WILEY
AUTHOR OF
"ALCESTIS," "THE COMING OF PHILIBERT," "CROMWELL," ETC.

New York
THE MACMILLAN COMPANY
LONDON: MACMILLAN & CO., LTD.
1909
All Rights Reserved

Copyright, 1909
The Macmillan Company

Set up, September, 1909.   Printed, October, 1909

THE SCIENTIFIC PRESS
ROBERT DRUMMOND AND COMPANY
NEW YORK

This scarce antiquarian book is included in our special *Legacy Reprint Series*. In the interest of creating a more extensive selection of rare historical book reprints, we have chosen to reproduce this title even though it may possibly have occasional imperfections such as missing and blurred pages, missing text, poor pictures, markings, dark backgrounds and other reproduction issues beyond our control. Because this work is culturally important, we have made it available as a part of our commitment to protecting, preserving and promoting the world's literature. Thank you for your understanding.

DANTE AND BEATRICE

THIS LITTLE VOLUME, HER FINAL WORK, IS A MEMORIAL
TO A BELOVED DAUGHTER, AND SEEMS A FITTING
CLOSE TO A LIFE DEVOTED TO THE SER-
VICE OF POETRY, A LIFE WHICH
ENNOBLED ALL WITH WHOM
SHE CAME IN CONTACT

INTRODUCTION

EVERY commanding personality has some one characteristic that colours all others, permeates all. In Sara Wiley Drummond, ardour was this quality. She seemed incarnate youth, one whose hope, energy, and fire could not be quenched by any weariness, or care, or grief. One purpose bound together all the diverse and eager interests of her life. Hers was the poet's great desire, hers the poet's noble satisfaction. With humility she moved, as was meet in the follower of great masters, and yet with dignity as a labourer in a high calling. Not for an instant did she doubt her task, and into it she threw an enthusiasm and a courage such as are never content with easy achievement.

Born to ease, she counted all the fair surroundings of life adjuncts, pleasant, at times powerful, but to be dismissed without a thought if need were. Her delight in luxuries was as candid as the enjoyment of a child, her indifference to them was superb.

She dwelt in a democracy of thought, beauty, righteousness. In the face of these, externals did not exist. To her were given those great gifts of the gods,—a childhood blithe and care free, a youth of ambition and glad endeavour, a marriage of full joy that closed in sorrow nobly borne and that bequeathed to her after years its perfect memory. With her own Dante she had said:

> "Courage is left, gallantly hour by hour
> To serve men and to save; the vivid earth
> Thrilling with song is left, the solemn hills,
> The restless flashing sea of fluctuant waves,
> The silver hosts of the assembled stars."

From such a life she won an outlook sane, and generous, and glad.

The intensity with which she worked and played gave to her accomplishment, whatever its nature, a speed that left the onlooker in amused astonishment. The scholarly temperament, the calm love of learning for its own sake, was not hers. She snatched her knowledge rather as the chosen men of Gideon quenched their thirst. Accuracy of impression and vividness of memory went with her strength of imagination and her instinct for essentials. For all the power of keen analysis, which she used upon herself after a curiously impersonal fashion, her point of view was thoroughly objective and her absorption in the matter of the moment, that led often to droll complications and to absurd misunderstandings, was an absorption not in herself, but in another or in an idea.

People filled her stage, and many lives far different from her own, and often in strange contrast, entered into her experience. Sincerity and an ideal, these these were the passports to her fellowship. Every meeting with a friend was an event laden with significance; every new acquaintance was an uncharted land holding forth rich promise to the explorer. To her extraordinary directness of approach even strangers yielded, knowing instinctively that behind her frank dealing lay no curiosity, no missionary attitude, no search for copy, but simple friendliness. The openness she surprised in others, that she returned, often with a childlike simplicity, since, in her view, what one learned of life was too precious and too hard won to be kept to one's self. She startled the conventional mind and left it wondering what manner of woman might this be, clearly sincere and earnest, she learned the difficult lesson of taking adverse criticism without flinching, and here she gained, and here beyond measure she gave, the inspiration that may come from generous intercourse with fellow-craftsmen. No trace of self-seeking or of vanity blinded her to the abilities of others. Rather she saw these greater than they were. She pinned her faith to the promise when the performance disappointed, and not alone in the days when all things are possible, or within that charmed circle of daring and happy youth, but everywhere and with everyone, after years had taught the commonness of failure, the irony of circumstance, she still divined brave powers in her fellows and urged them ever on toward a golden future.

To her friends she dealt indeed something of the faith and admiration she had given the heroes of her school days. She was essentially a hero-worshipper, one whose heroes were set firmly in their places, and were never crowded out by later enthusiasms. Brutus and Cromwell embodied her love of liberty and her zest for action. Dante and Milton were the prophet-poets, but they were quite as truly types of the grandeur of human pain. Such were her chosen company and for her some kinship with these great examples now and again lifted a contemporary quite beyond the cavil of observers more critical or more influenced by those details that the future ignores.

This enthusiasm for others, whether personal friends or historic figures, marked her writings as it marked her daily doings. There is a vigour and a scope in *Cromwell*, the work of the school-girl, that shows it of another genus than the easy lyric writing of verse-makers whose own emotions are the warp and woof of their frail web of song. In this her living and her writing were of one nature. It was the eager grasp of experience beyond her own that cast her poems more and more into the dramatic form, that taught her so brave and so fine a notion of the personal responsibility alike of women and of men for the common weal, and that endowed her with so wise and unfailing a sympathy.

Nothing ever entered calmly or with indifferent effect into her life, and religion, always real to her, grew with her years, more and more vital to all her thinking. Her reverent ambition, the writing of a Christian hymn, was never realized, not because she was, as she deemed herself, yet untrained for the high task, but for a reason deeper and indeed quite other. Expression in words she had found a spontaneous and inevitable outlet for the more grave and beautiful emotions of life. Yet religion with her was most of all a matter of conduct. The inner impulse expressed itself, not in meditation, but in results; not in the inward and direct communion of the soul with God, but in the practice of mutual brotherhood. A common righteousness was her instinctive need. So, though more real and immediate to her than the incidents of daily intercourse, was this sense of the infinite source and the infinite destiny of the human soul, yet she had not that hunger for the direct communion which is precisely the inspiration of the religious poem.

Slender and tall she stood, her head crowned with ruddy brown hair that waved and curled, a mist about her face. Her lips and eyes changed momently with her changing thought. The rhythm of her tread and of her gesture was born in her, with her sense of the cadence of words. Her beauty was singularly a beauty bound up with personality, and seldom does human form so perfectly express the flaming spirit within. Intensely and completely one with her fellows, she yet gave, even to those who met her casually, a vision of a more generous and mightier world wherein she dwelt. When the word came that she, in whom life was so vivid, so tireless, so instinct with youth, had gone swiftly into the great silence, it struck with a sense of bitter desolation, of irremediable loss, so wide and varied a group as may seldom be reached by life of a few years and of no public service. Four slender volumes hold all that work in letters to which she set herself at once solemnly and joyously. Her art developed slowly, but it grew steadily and surely and to-day, as we read the *Dante and Beatrice*, which she laid by in her last week, we know that with her passing went not only a woman of extraordinary charm, but a poet whose words were of significance and beauty ever increasing.

E. W. B.

DANTE AND BEATRICE

CHARACTERS

Dante Alighieri
Folco Portinari
Corso Donati
Forese Donati
Simone dei Bardi
Guido Cavalcanti
Cino da Pistoia
Cecco Angiolieri
Casella
Beatrice Portinari
Piccarda Donati
Gemma Donati

Two nuns, nobles and ladies, men-at-arms and servants.

The scene is at Florence, between the years 1283 and 1290.

DANTE AND BEATRICE

ACT I

SCENE I

Beside the Arno.

Corso *and* Forese Donati *enter*.

CORSO
This vapouring of death that is not death,
And life in love of God, will drive me soon
To prove the body real by violence
Enacted. Brother, I am solid flesh,
Moved by desire and quickened by my blood;
No moonsick musings of a virgin's dream
Balks me of my set purpose.

FORESE
            Nay, but, Corso,
She is too frail a plant for rough-blown winds.

CORSO

Let her be obedient, then will I be mild.
I shall hold Florence yet and all this land,
Shall I not dominate one maiden's whim
And rule my family who rule the state?

FORESE

I wish that Dante stood with us—

CORSO

                        Not I!
Another dreamer of the intangible.

FORESE

He is my closest friend.

CORSO

                 That is thy folly.

FORESE

On his strong wisdom learning, like a cloak
Heavy with broidery, is lightly borne.

Act I   **Dante and Beatrice**

CORSO

Here is our cousin Gemma, out of breath.
                               [GEMMA *enters*.

GEMMA

My lords, where is Piccarda?

CORSO
                 Do I know?
Praying in her convent.

GEMMA
             Not an hour since
She left the house in haste to follow you.

FORESE

Why comes she from the convent?

GEMMA
                  Make me not
The unwelcome bearer of ill-tidings, sir.

CORSO

If she hath come to say she takes the veil
It shall hang heavy with a brother's curse.

GEMMA

Say not I told you.

FORESE

     We will lure the dove
Forth from her cage and in the sunny air
Toss her to use her wings.

GEMMA

      There is one voice
Only in Florence, that will summon her.
Dante can move her. Let us send for him.

CORSO

Many have called me honey-tongued, more skilled
In speech than Dante.

GEMMA

    Let us judge of that.

FORESE

He will take her part.

GEMMA
Not if I plead with him.

CORSO
You think you sway him when he smiles at you,
My pretty Vanity!

GEMMA
He yields to me.

FORESE
He is the courtliest man in Florence.

CORSO
                              No.
He is praised of listening ladies whom he scorns.

GEMMA
No, never scorns.

FORESE
But never follows.

GEMMA

                  No.
Here is Piccarda. She is as pale as wax.
      [PICCARDA *enters, in the habit of a novice,
      with her, two nuns.*

PICCARDA

My gentle brothers—

CORSO

              If you seek for us
In duty and in fit humility,
Come home, Piccarda, but if that proud spirit
Rule in you still—

FORESE

        Have you forgot your sex?

CORSO

Silence. I spoke, the head of the house. Piccarda,
You are dishonest.

PICCARDA

Sir!

Act I   Dante and Beatrice

7

CORSO
You are a thief!
A woman is the treasure of her house,
Wherewith to purchase glory and estate.

PICCARDA
Dear brother, I was God's ere I was yours.

GEMMA
Do not be heavenly, you will anger him.

PICCARDA
If Dante, my dear friend, could plead for me
He should speak silver words.

CORSO
                    Why have you come?
I want no silver, steel is my weapon. Speak.

PICCARDA
How shall I tell of the far, starry hosts
To you, whose obdurate, dull gaze is fixed
Forever on the clods and stones of earth.

8

By months of passionate prayer and holy vigil
I have come to live no more after the flesh.
My days are consecrated and redeemed,
My heart elate with pure ecstatic joys,
My soul attuned to an eternal love,
And I must wake and sleep, even until death
With Him, my Heavenly Spouse.

FORESE

                Where would you go?

PICCARDA

To veil and clothe me by the rule of Clare.
I will not lead your life that ends in death.

CORSO

Death? It is death you seek, unthankful girl.
But you shall live, and live to do my will.
Go to your convent. When I find the man
Shall bring to us and you favour and wealth,
I will hale you from your altars by the hair
And change your sterile vows for marriage bonds.

PICCARDA
Lost, all our souls unto eternal death!
           [She faints.

CORSO
Death!

FORESE
 Death!
     [DANTE *enters, crossing the bridge.*

DANTE
   Death! Who calls on death in spring,
When every perfumed breeze gent'y calls love?
Why breaks a discord on the season's tune,
This keening cry of cranes that blot the sun?
Doth any soul pass from the friendly earth
Quitting the light for measureless grey air?
          [He approaches.
Not fair Piccarda, loved of early flowers?

FORESE
Dante, she is not dead, a wind of wrath
Has quelled the torch, it will revive again

The brighter, for her spirit is unquenched.
She goes to bind herself to the poor Clares
Against our will.

DANTE
            As rivers seek the sea
She moves within the encircling will of God
That draws all wills to Him and makes them His.
Corso, forbear. Be comforted, Forese,
And let your little sister go in peace.

PICCARDA
It is not death I crave, but love divine,
And even you, my master, know it not.

GEMMA
Just now she looks as if she knew as well
An earthly love.

DANTE
            Hush, Gemma. Messer Corso,
Bring no discredit on your house and name
By violence to the church. This is an honour
To you and yours. Let her go quietly.

Act I   **Dante and Beatrice**

II

CORSO
Dante Alighieri, I am not schooled
By you, though you are learned.

DANTE
                I am patient.

FORESE
That you are never.   Brother, offend him not.
Go quickly, sister.

DANTE
God be with you, child.

PICCARDA
May the sweet dew of heavenly thoughts rain down
Refreshment and cool comfort on your souls.
                [*She goes, with nuns.*

CORSO
Come, Gemma, here the air is too fine for us.
I would you were my sister.

GEMMA

    Sirs, farewell.
              [They go.

FORESE

Dreams are not dainties, I will not feed on them.
Give me the juicy meat of passion and war,
Delicate cakes of dalliance, foaming wines
Of kisses; I am for joyance and quick life.
You waste your days in a deep mystery.
Now, as you cast those pebbles, one by one,
They sink into the Arno and are lost.

DANTE

The circles break and break, running away
Till the smooth, level river stirs and trembles.

FORESE

Why do the women of Florence sigh for you?
You are *the courteous Dante*, I know not what—
You draw them by a charm men cannot fathom,
A grace of wisdom. Yet you never loved.

13

Tell me the secret of your flinty heart:
You are poor, not great, not famous, you might wed
And mend your fortune.

DANTE

                Can the world give more
Than the liberty to labour and to love?

FORESE

Ally your learning to a noble house,
Riches, estates, and be a prince indeed.

DANTE

One who had empire said nobility
Was courteous bearing and an ancient wealth.

FORESE

It is to enter life in palace gates,
To grow amid the fostering strength of gold,
A splendid plant set in a fertile soil;
To rest in age upon a velvet throne,
Admired, adored and envied of the mean.

14

DANTE

I think not so it is: a youth of grace
Whose bright cheeks flush with wonder of the wor
Manhood, a warrior serving loyally;
Age that rejoices in all excellence,
A husbandman, whose garner deep with grain,
The affluent fruitage of laborious years,
Dispenses plenteous wisdom to mankind.

FORESE

Whoso hath riches holds the world in fee.

DANTE

Riches are base; by undiscerning chance
Augmented, following nor wisdom nor worth,
Bestowing not nobility; their loss
Detracts no honour from an upright mind.
Their growth is hazardous, possession breeds
Mistrust and mischief, for an anxious care
Is needful to their gain, and who is sage
Directs his labours to a lordlier end.
" Alas, what wretch," says old Boethius,

"Dug from reluctant earth these precious perils?"
Nobility abides where virtue is,
There is the heaven wherever is the star.

FORESE

You honour virtue with a lover's tongue.
What woman makes your garden paradise?

DANTE

No woman, friend.

FORESE

    Well then, what mystic dream?
Some fancy is here.

DANTE

    If I have never told
Through my own wish, I shall not speak through yours.
Bicci Novello, your ill-fated Nella
Would counsel none to wed.

FORESE

    She is too devout!

DANTE
You are a fine advocate of wedlock!

FORESE
                        Yes.
I hold so many keys and know all wards.

DANTE
Hush, for there is a benison on this morn,
The air of Eden, of the new-born world
Scented with gracile blossoms dew-besprent.
    [BEATRICE, *with two ladies, comes upon the bridge.*

FORESE
Lo, your fair neighbour, gentle Beatrice!
You never look on women, now you are hanging
Over the bridge to see your own swart face.
    [DANTE *lifts his head,* BEATRICE *salutes
    him and passes.*

DANTE
These are white angels, spirits of the light.
One is the Dawn and one, I think, is Spring,

And she, most beautiful, is very Love.
I could forget all miseries and harms,
Pardon all trespasses. Humility
Has bent me to the earth, but the pale dust
Is sown with fragrant flowers.

FORESE

        Even unto me
The air grew clearer and the earth serene
And life more gentle as she saluted us.

DANTE

I have seen the sum of human blessedness,
My heart is running over with joy and peace,
O, love and love—love! All the universe
Throbs to the chanting of the eternal song.

FORESE

Dante!

DANTE

  Earth changes. The new life begins.

SCENE II

The hall in the house of SIMONE DEI BARDI. *Servants pass to and fro. Guests enter,* CASELLA *among them,* CORSO *and* FORESE DONATI. DANTE *enters.*

FORESE

Here is the poet and the cavalier
Of many lyrics and of many ladies!
I was deceived that morning on the bridge.
I thought that Folco Portinari's pearl
Had made you covetous, and you wrote her songs
That set us all a-weeping. Fickle fancy
Blows an uncertain gust on windmill lovers
Round you swing, amorous of Lagia, next,
Chanting her praise.

DANTE

Will Gemma come to-night?

CORSO

Two is not enough! Cry welcome to a third!
She is here and brings Piccarda.

Act I   Dante and Beatrice

DANTE
              From her convent?

CORSO
No more of convents! She is already a bride.

FORESE
It was not my wish, Dante, but Corso's will.

DANTE
Cold heart and coward, Forese!

FORESE
              Nay. The man
Is rich and noble and loves her.

DANTE
              Who is he?

CORSO
It is Rossellino della Tosa.

DANTE
          You
Chose him for your advantage, yielding her
Who is so exquisite and soft a thing,
Into his violent and treacherous hands
With less of hesitation or regret
Than you would feel in parting with cold coin.

FORESE
But Rossellino—

DANTE
          A bat-faced libertine!

CORSO
Sir, mend your speech!

FORESE
          Remember where you are!

DANTE
[*To* CORSO] Now may God smite you for this ravish-
        ment!
And may I see you dragged to nether hell,

Befouled until you lose the face of man
And look at last the carrion that you are!

FORESE

Strike him not, Corso! Look, Piccarda comes.
[CORSO *and* FORESE *withdraw*. PICCARDA,
entering, goes to DANTE.

PICCARDA

Brother, my only brother, I am lost.
I am damned already.

DANTE

    Alas, poor little dove
By obscene vultures torn! Poor frightened child!

PICCARDA

Because I suffer so much, think you that God
Will yet forgive my sin?

DANTE

     Look in my face;
Do I not pity thee?

PICCARDA

Because you love me.

DANTE

Doth not God love thee more, pity thee more,
And deeplier know thy gentle, sinless heart?
There is no stain on thy white robe, Piccarda,
And thou shalt beam a pearl in Paradise.
Torn by man's wrath from the sweet cloister's shade,
Thou hast not loosed the veil that shrouds thy heart,
Thou art espoused to the Great Primal Lover.
Thy will in union with the will of God
Is perfect still.

PICCARDA

And His will is our peace.
May God so comfort you in your sore need
As I am comforted.

[*She goes.*

DANTE

I could slay Corso
With these lean fingers. He is like a cat

Act I   Dante and Beatrice

That bears away a tiny piping bird
Whose cries grow fainter as the teeth clutch in.
            [CECCO ANGIOLIERI, CINO DA PISTOIA *and*
                GUIDO CAVALCANTI *enter*.

CECCO

Cecco, your comrade, begs you, by that love
We serve alike in rags and wrath, to say
If I, that love and lack the gallant gold,
May not as well go hang myself?

DANTE
                        Not so,
Why cheat an honest hangman of his job?
                        [GEMMA *enters*.

GEMMA

Tell us, good Cecco, if your cobbler's girl
Goes barefoot?

CECCO

    It is the fairest foot unshod.

GEMMA
Her father makes for Messer Adimari
Egregious points, and he with toes outspread
Blocks San Martini as he rides along.

CECCO
I know he makes a sharp point on his shoes.

GEMMA
He points thy jests perhaps with just such points.

CECCO
Becchina beckons me to appoint a point
Where beak and beak may meet.

GEMMA
                       On beaker's brim?
Your cobbler fits your wit with seven-league boots!
Yet on the earth still must you stamp along,
While Dante flies on wings of poesy.

FORESE
My merry cousin loves the solemn singer.

GEMMA
You will see at last the current of his life
Steal down from distant hills to meet with mine.

FORESE
He loves bright Beatrice.

GEMMA
     —A mystic rapture
Unutterable and born of dewy dreams
Dissolved before the dawn. He will speak not
The word that wins the heart; or he will speak
Too late, when agony has loosed his tongue.

FORESE
I cannot understand. You are a woman
Who seeks the quiet nook, the homely task,
Nor learning, nor great songs, nor clamorous fame
Can please you.

GEMMA
    No, I do not care for these.
Yet he is wine to me. One summer day

I saw him soothe a weary little child
With murmured tales; and once, beside a fount,
Whose purling spray shivered the green and gold
Pool, to swift silver serpents travelling,
I heard him teach a prattling group to sing
Ave Maria, and he smiled and praised
Their voices while they clung about his knees.

CINO

[*To* DANTE] Hail, poet of death and love!

DANTE

                        I thank you, Cino,
For answer to my song.

CINO

                Guessed I aright,
That Love would have you show your lady your heart
And therefore fed her with it who had lain
Long in uncaring sleep, and that he wept
Pitying her for the terrible joy and sweet
That stirred within her bosom?

DANTE
                  I cannot tell.

CECCO
Then, if you cannot tell, why does your Muse
Lead us like marshfire such a twirl of rhymes
To plump us in the mud of ignorance?

DANTE
You are unlearned in love.

CECCO
                  I am sadly wise;
When I behold Becchina in a rage
I quail as a poor boy whose master lifts
And flourishes a stinging rod. And yet
I could survive without this love. I am not
Penned in his hutch, my spirits are too quick.
I fly from anything that makes men glum
And carves their faces peaked.

DANTE
                  Autumn oak
Like thine, good Cecco, changes not to pine!

28

CECCO
An overdose of love makes fools.

DANTE
                              Thy brain
Hath yielded to a very little dose.

CECCO
We will not kick our nettles, brother ass,
But save them for our fodder prudently.
You scorn my pretty sonnets to Becchina,
Your cockerel crows too high for such a hen.
I am a poor devil, quick to love or hate,
—Done with repentance, where is the good of that?
Now, when I itch I scratch, and there is an end!—
Hoping for idle days and merry mates.
You bear your nose so high, I wish you would trip!

CAVALCANTI
[*To* CINO] Present me, pray, to Messer Alighieri.

CINO
Sweet Messer Dante, here is a brother poet.

DANTE

O honoured Cavalcanti, this bright hour
Shall be red-marked forever, yet not to-day
I greet you first; our Muses met and kissed
Wandering together in the mazy rhyme.
Your gentle answer to my sonnet, sir,
Makes me your friend.

CAVALCANTI

                Read I your riddle aright?
I do beseech you, say it now to me.

DANTE

To every sweet soul that in chains doth move,
   And every presence where this song shall be,
   For the unveiling of its mystery
Be salutation in our Lord, even Love.
Whenas a third of the star-bright hours above
   Across the shadowy dome fled silently,
   Love on a sudden was revealed to me,
At whose aspect my life and terror strove.

My heart within his hand, joyous he came,
And lightly bore my lady on his arm
Enfolded in a mantle, while she slept;
He wakened her and of that heart of flame
Humbly she ate as one that feareth harm,
Then he went on his way, and going wept.

CAVALCANTI

Thou didst behold the sum of blessedness
Given to men to know. Lest she should die
When thou didst love, that righteous Lord of life
Fed her upon thy heart. Have then no fear
Although he seemed to go in sadness forth,
Thou knowest in dreams we see the truth reversed.

DANTE

Yet there are hours when, pondering frail life,
How brief it is, Love waileth in my breast,
And once, by day, methought the sun grew dim
And the delicate stars trembled and shed bright tears;
Swift birds fell dead. And then I saw ascend
Angels innumerable in glorious song
That bore a little cloud, whiter than fleece.

I heard afar long, sobbing lamentations,
And came at last where Beatrice lay, immaculate
And mild in death, and Death himself seemed blessed.
And while fair ladies swathed her in a veil,
Methought I heard the murmur of her lips,
I am at peace. I strove to call her name,
And as I struggled, woke in strangling tears.

CAVALCANTI

Since you have spoken of her, forbid me not
To ask if still she rules you.

DANTE

     Yea, forever.
Brother of mine, look on the heart thou holdest.
I could not have rude men, inquisitive, watch,
To mark how love assailed me, and I paled
And tremours shook me from the very heart
Whenas I gazed and drew life from her face.
So, as I lately saw near Beatrice
A damozel who thought I gazed on her
And smiled thereat, straightway I made of her

My screen and let men think she had enthralled me.
Thus have I loved my heart's fill unbeheld.
                    [CAVALCANTI *withdraws*.

FORESE

Why will you herd with cattle like that man,
The most outrageous of the Ghibellines
And no fit friend for any friend of mine?
A spiggot, a proud stick, my brother says.
Corso has taken oath to murder him
And any other of his company.

DANTE

Is this a threat, Forese?

FORESE

            No, dear Dante,
Only a prayer that you forsake his speech.
He is the foremost of our enemies,
A scoffer, and, men whisper, atheist.

DANTE

Good servant of the Church! My pious friend!

FORESE
I am no saint, but yet no heretic.
He walks at eventide among the graves
Behind the Baptistry, saying strange words,
Blasphemous, touching our immortality.
Such men as he should burn here and hereafter.

DANTE
He is a poet.

FORESE
          That is no praise to me.
It is an injury to our close love
For you to turn and follow troubadours.
I will not hear you say you are a poet,
Who could be formidable and supreme
In state and camp. Leave word-plays to the weak.

DANTE
Now you are blasphemous. I do not wish
For other laurels than the poet's bays.
A wondrous tremour shakes me from the heart.
My senses sink. I live within my eyes.
         [BEATRICE *enters with* PORTINARI.

34

Lo, how she beams above the sombre world
Like a pale star set in the purple sky,
Or like a lily on a dusky lake!

FORESE

Men press to gaze upon her, and all speech
Trembles to silence, every glance abased
Before her purity. She walks serene
Haloed and garmented with humbleness.

DANTE

When I behold thy face, Puissant Joy,
My thoughts break with the exultancy of love.
> [BEATRICE *passes.* DANTE *bows before
her, but she does not return his salutation.*

DANTE

Ah, God of Mercy, she denies me blessing!
Take me away, my frail soul faints in me.

FORESE

Nay, die not yet, sweet Dante, not of this.
Die in ripe years of fever or the plague,

In lusty youth smiting a mighty foe
Fall gallantly, but never faint and fail
Before a maiden's little frown, or I
Shall die a-laughing. Hold thy head up, man!

PORTINARI

Give me your arm, my daughter, I must rest.
My breath comes like a stag's pursued by hounds.
                                                [*He sits.*
Young Dante wrote fine verses to you, girl,
And will you not salute him who so loves you?

BEATRICE

Does he so love me, sir? He praises Lagia,
Until men talk of it past courtesy,
And she is sore distressed.

PORTINARI
                I am content.
Poets are as fickle as the sweet airs of song,
They string their lutes with many an idle love.
Yet be not cruel. Should the sun not shine
Because the nightingale praises the moon?

BEATRICE

I know that Dante loves me; I rebuked him
Because he does not well to trouble Lagia.

PORTINARI

That is no near concern of yours, my child.
Come here beside me. Let us speak awhile
Of Dante, whom your scorn makes miserable,
For I have feared that love of poesy
And all such sweets and trifles, drew you on
To over-pay a thousand-fold those rhymes.
You have discernment; who is always wise?
Trust me, my dear, I would not do as some
Thrifty, who profit by their beauteous daughters.
You shall be happy. I will seek your choice
As far as loving wisdom may permit,
Nor force your inclination. As for Dante,
I have inquired of him. He is not for thee.
What hath he done to merit such a crown?
Men of his age have been renowned in war.

BEATRICE

He is a poet, sir.

Act I   **Dante and Beatrice**

PORTINARI
           You are a dreamer!
Will singing feed you sweet and clothe you soft,
As you are accustomed? He might turn his rhymes
And yet be illustrious, as some have been.
His life drifts onward, a meandering stream
That dallies through low meadows, wanting urge
Of valiant rivers plunging to the main.
I value high emprise of poesy.
Were he ten times a poet, yet a man
That thou couldst trust safely to care for thee,
Still shouldst thou have him, dearest Beatrice.
I love thee past the love of any man,
  Lover or husband. Do I not wish thy joy?
Would I not buy it with my reddest blood?

BEATRICE
Father, my days have been all sunshine.

PORTINARI
                           Sweet,
I love thee far too well to see thee suffer,

I must protect thee from thine innocent self.
Let me judge for thee.   Am I not reckoned wise?

BEATRICE

Most wise, most generous.

PORTINARI

            Then trust to me.

BEATRICE

Did you not wed for love?

PORTINARI

            Yea, for great love,
And found great happiness.

BEATRICE

            Then is not love
The road to happiness?

PORTINARI

            A love like ours,
Mine and your mother's: but this is not so,

This is pure fantasy of two wild brains.
You must have merry days. Behold that face!
Could he be ever cheerful?

     BEATRICE
    He has wit.

     PORTINARI
It may be so: but has he happiness?
I tell thee that his face is marked for sorrow.
He will suffer always.

     BEATRICE
    Who shall comfort him?

     PORTINARI
Alas, poor pitiful child, what could you do
But wreck yourself upon a rocky fate?
    [GEMMA *and other ladies approach.*

     GEMMA
[*To* BEATRICE] You have slain him by your coldness.

FIRST LADY
                              Like a bow
His mouth curves downward as you draw the string.

SECOND LADY

For all our sakes, one glimpse of April sun
On Dante, to dispel the thunder-cloud
Before the cream within the larder sours!

GEMMA

Dante da Majano has sent a song
To Messer Alighieri on his dream:
He begged him to take physic and seek out
A leech to cure him of his malady
Of nightmare.   And I thought it sage advice.

FORESE

They are all mocking you.   Beatrice laughs.

DANTE

No man was ever stricken as am I.

FIRST LADY

Dante!

DANTE

What would you of your slave, Madonna?

FIRST LADY

Why lovest thou this lady and canst not suffer
Even her presence? I pray thee come and tell.
Certes, the wish of such a love is strange.

DANTE

O ladies mine, in her sweet salutation,
The goal of love and my beatitude,
Lay the fulfillment of desire, but since
She who is ever of a courtesy
Ineffable denies it, Love, my lord,
Hath placed my blessing where it cannot fail.

FIRST LADY

Alas, what sorrow is his!

SECOND LADY

What love he bears!

THIRD LADY

Woe is me, I would one loved me so.

FIRST LADY

                                    Beseech thee,
Tell us, wherein abideth now thy blessing?

DANTE

Even in these words of mine that honour her.

THIRD LADY

If this were so then wouldst thou speak and praise her.

DANTE

Ladies that have intelligence of love,
Whose graciousness constrains my burdened heart
To rise and flow as the moon lifts the sea,
I may not fitly praise the lady I love,
It is a theme too lofty. When I muse
Upon her virtue, love such sweetness sheds
About me, that my blossoming songs are closed.
If I should speak all men must turn to love.

GEMMA

Love and the gentle heart are the same thing,
Therefore we join with thee to honour her.

DANTE

As crystal dew ascends to meet the sun,
So might the beams of heaven withdraw her soul.
An angel in celestial wisdom prays,
" Lord, on the earth a radiant miracle
Shines even to us, and every saint implores
Her spirit to complete the bliss of heaven."

FIRST LADY

Dante, pray thou that she abide on earth.

SECOND LADY

God will have pity on thee who dread her loss.

DANTE

Should I descend to hell, I yet could say,
" I saw the hope of those that dwell in bliss."

GEMMA
A fragrance breathes about her on the air,
And when we look upon her perfect face,
Modest and winsome, unaware we sigh.

FIRST LADY
Beauty is proved by her.

THIRD LADY
How chanceth it
That mortal thing should be so undefiled?

DANTE
Go with her, each of you who would be blessed,
For where she passes evil shrinks rebuked,
And all uncomely thoughts are frozen and chilled,
As noxious weeds beneath the silver snow:
Whoso can look upon her loveliness
Must either be ennobled or else must die.
            [*The ladies pass,* GEMMA *remains.*

GEMMA

You are like a pilgrim seeking through the hills
Amid sharp cold and over the steep stones
A flower inaccessible; in warm valleys
The plentiful roses flush and fade ungathered.

DANTE

The eagle soars against the burning sun
A wanderer and a warrior of the sky,
Not long he crouches in the swaying nest,
His pathway is beyond the eternal snows
In crystal air.

GEMMA

    Some day his wings will weary.

FORESE

[*To* DANTE] I will go to her and plead for thee.
    Take heart.
                    [*He crosses to* BEATRICE.
Madonna, beauty should be merciful,

May not poor Dante come and speak with thee
And be forgiven?   Almost he faints for grief.
      [SIMONE DEI BARDI *enters*.

PORTINARI

[*To* BEATRICE] There is a man whose heart is like
 a fount
Of sunlit waters, plenteous and clear,
And well he loves you.   Mark how men salute him.

SIMONE

Incomparable Beatrice, I see
No face but thine; thy brightness dims the throng
As the fair moon subdues the twinkling stars.

FORESE

Will not the queen set free her prisoner
In honour of this feast?

BEATRICE

  Bid Dante come.
      [DANTE *approaches*.

SIMONE

Welcome, Sir Poet! I have read your songs
And liked them well.

DANTE

You are most complaisant,
Messer dei Bardi. [*To* PORTINARI] I salute you, sir.
[*To* BEATRICE] Madonna, is it your will I speak with
   you?

SIMONE

Let us withdraw; the poor soul is distressed,
Tongue-tied before us. Cruel Beatrice!
   [FORESE, SIMONE *and* PORTINARI *withdraw*.

DANTE

If thou shouldst know my state thou wouldst not
   mock
With other ladies; rather, pity me.
Madonna, Love himself will plead my cause
Saying, " His faith is firm, early was yours,
And never faltered. If his humble prayer
For grace displeases you, command him then

To die, and your poor servant shall obey."
I am blind, bewildered, stricken. Give me hope!
A blighting frost blackens and bows to earth
My every flower.

                BEATRICE
           You are forgiven, sir.

                DANTE
Most blessed lady, in whom alone love dwells,
Thy healing mercy hath assuaged my pain.
Surely love pleaded for me while I wept.

                BEATRICE
I would have you be as great as God hath willed,
And therefore can I not endure a stain
Upon his glorious handiwork.

                DANTE
                    Tear forth
Anything in me that offends, though life
Run from the wound.

PORTINARI

      You are wise, though young, Simone.
I long to rest and think the world of men
Well-doing and gentle. I would live at ease
And have no shocks nor changes. Weariness
Is the dull opiate of cunning Death
To numb the victim. I must think and act,
Nor sleep before my night while work is to do.
I know you loved your sister. In her marriage
Has she found joy, and did she choose to wed?

SIMONE

Surely, good Messer Folco, she is happy.
You could not th'nk I asked a maid her fancies?
Women have less than we of strength and will.
It is ours to shelter them, to smooth their path,
To guide them steadily.

PORTINARI

      True; but with love.

SIMONE

The love that rules and cherishes. The maid
Whose musing soars not past the broidered scene
She fashions and deems life, quits not her father
Till her strong husband lifts her o'er his threshold.
The hearts of women are our sanctuary,
We seek the perfume of the sheltered close
From dust and rain and lightning on the road.

PORTINARI

You are as sage as men have reckoned you,
Yet sometimes when my Bice reads, and lifts
Her eyes, thought-litten, murmuring great words
Of ancient song, I doubt my mastery.

SIMONE

She dwells in heaven and no rude voice of earth
Should break upon the music echoing there.
You do not think that she could choose a spouse
By any precept learned in Paradise?
We know what all men are—the best—but she
Must think no evil or our joy were lost.

She is submissive and her heart will follow
Where you have chosen.

PORTINARI
       You are young, Simone.

DANTE
[*To* BEATRICE] Your smile is light that shining from within
Illumes the windows of your happy eyes.

BEATRICE
I have lived like a flower blown in the sun,
Yet the wind whispers of the distant waves,
And the stars beacon to mysterious skies:
For I will tell you of my solemn dreams
That hand in hand with God I serve His world;
Faithful I labour at the lesser things
Of woman's work, but my dream is to serve,
Not when I sit and weave among my maids,
Not when I smile and pass through crowded ways,
But with the giving of my eager heart
The life of me, the spirit I had from God.

How shall I find the way?   You only know—
You are not as other men.   There is in you
A splendour of purple hills that touch the sky,
A vastness like the spaces of the sea.

DANTE

Thou liftest up thy mouth for bread of angels,
Earth cannot satisfy nor earth retain
Thy spirit; thou shalt tread the path of stars
Amidst the music of eternal joy.
None unrewarded ever prayed to serve
The needy world.   Thou shalt restore our faith.
Pure, beaming mirror of celestial light,
Beholding thee men are aware of God
Who only could have made thee as thou art.

BEATRICE

Speak to me of yourself: you shall be famed.

DANTE

Seldom are gathered from Apollo's tree
The leaves wherewith my temples shall be crowned,

Act I   **Dante and Beatrice**

There in my beautiful San Giovanni
Within the ancient Baptistry, where once
My life was given to Christ. I shall not lose
In earth's dim labyrinth the love of Him.
Holding that golden clue my steps may pass,—
Leaving the camps of Guelf or Ghibelline,
Contemned, reviled, perhaps by foes cast forth,—
To abandon all I cherish, and to know
How salt doth taste another's bread, how steep
The passage up and down another's stairs:
Driven to seek a refuge in the wilds,
To toil by narrow cleft and precipice,
Sheltered in caves, and crouched on frosty turf;
Amidst the nests of vipers and the dens
Of unclean beasts of prey my nights may be.
Albeit I set me square against the stroke
Of fortune, and my cry shall be a wind
Smiting the loftiest summits. Unafraid
I shall endure all things, if so I serve
My beauteous Florence, glorious child of Rome.
And that great nation that shall be, come down
Like New Jerusalem, sceptred and crowned
With lilies, robed in silver, and adorned

With ornaments of gold, shall honour me
Forever and forever—make my name
One with those names that beam as the fixed stars,
For unto me is given the power of God,
To mould a world that of itself lives on.
And I shall shed my blood to make men strong,
Breathe in their nostrils my immortal spirit,
Make them the heirs of the rich heritage
Of wisdom purchased by my agony.
For what is my ambition? Not for that
Grasped by the hand or visible to the eyes.
I shall interpret the marred manuscript
And ancient signs of man's mysterious heart,
And at the centre of the universe
Show him Primæval Love toward which he moves.
The power descends, my veins are sluiced with fire,
My labouring heart pants to break through my flesh:
This is the thirst that parched lean Cæsar's lips,
Wrung Alexander's tears, slew Socrates;
This is the rowel to the speeding horse
That forges toward the goal; this is the cup
That scatters fervid poison and honey-dew!
The tinkling coinage of my trivial days

Act I   Dante and Beatrice

55

I will scatter like a largess at the feet
Of destiny, if I may speak and live.

BEATRICE

May the proud spirits of the glorious dead
Companion thee, and fill thy soul with song,
Investing with their vanished potency
The mind that follows the immortal train,
Hallow and liberate thy struggling heart,
Rouse thee to courage and to constancy,
Blow like the wind that quickens burning coal
Till that great flame, the love of beauty, rise,
Consume thy dross and leave thee child of God.
And let me serve thee any way I may.
Art thou so far above thou canst not hear?

DANTE

Most beautiful, you are with me now and ever.
                                        [*Music.*
The music floats above the clamorous hall,
A gentle angel breathing benison.
Hark, to the call of the clear viol!—Now
Accord and blend the sweet, united strains.

They will declare what tongue hath never told,
And my lips long for, never to attain,
Because it is a word of heaven, that earth
Hears echoing beyond, and shall not speak
Till mortal reaches immortality.

BEATRICE

The melody passes; a summer breeze
Bending the wheat in undulant, long lines,
Pauses in sudden eddying and sweeps on.

SIMONE

[*To* CASELLA] Messer Casella, will you charm our ears
With the joy of music?

CASELLA

      Gladly, at your pleasure.
(*Sings*) *Love in my mind a mighty music wakes,*
 And yearning unto him my voice I raise
 Impassioned to declare my lady's praise.
  'Mid mystic measures intricate and sweet,

57

My dazed thought its perilous passage takes,
  Rapt into rare and unaccustomed ways;
  Alas, my stricken sense no strength essays
    To attain and lay my worship at her feet.
    For who shall soar on seraph pinion fleet
Weighted with clogs of dull humanity?
Through mortal lips the vision of blessed eyes,
    Seek to immortalize,
A beauty unbeheld of all that see?
  Let censure fall alone on my oblation,
Whose rhymes reach not my lady's high degree.
  For mind is sunk in spirit's adoration,
And speech may never with such influence move
As shall command the harmonies of love.

DANTE

This is a prelude of a song to be
Wherein I set a crown about my brow
In honouring my friend, for like loves like.
Love is a glory bright through every veil,
Love is a song that thrills the silent air,
Love is a spring that overflows the shores,

58

Love is a fire consuming barriers,
Not to be stayed, nor silenced, nor concealed;
My face and life display it, and so, my song.
Still is unutterable the exalted theme—
The mystic union of the aspiring soul
With the beloved, yearning unto her
Whose radiance rains flamelets like the sun
Cheering the heaven: and though this passion rose
Contemplative of living loveliness,
Yet is she symbol of that heavenly wisdom
Sent us by Christ, who gave therewith His peace.

PORTINARI

Let us return, they have talked long enough.
       [FORESE *joins them as they return to*
          BEATRICE. DANTE *crosses to* CASELLA
          and CAVALCANTI.

DANTE

Casella mine, I take thee to my heart,
Thou stillest all desire.

Act I   Dante and Beatrice

CASELLA
I love thy song.

PORTINARI
[*To* FORESE] This Messer Alighieri is your friend?

FORESE
Since many years, but for how many more
I dare not say. You and I, Messer Folco,
Are men of reason, that man is a poet
And so, forsooth, would turn aside from us
To choose strange company; nor be content
With generous earth, but struggle up toward heaven
A pitiful inch beyond us, or dive down
Some way toward hell, or pry beneath men's lids
Haply to spy their souls. We see enough
In the bright visible world we tread, say I,
Enough to touch and seize and feed upon,
But poets are all moods—like a wild day
That storms, shines, blusters, woos, all in an hour.
I am out of patience with him—yet I love him.
                                           [*He goes.*

PORTINARI
[*To* BEATRICE] You hear: and this man is his closest
    friend!
Our host entreats your hand to open the dance.

BEATRICE
I do not wish such honour.

PORTINARI
                Take his hand
And take his heart, my child, this is the man
Whom I would see you wed. Start not away
With such a glance of terror, like a fawn
Quivering at gaze before the hounds. Dei Bardi
Loves you and says he loves you; comes to me
With honourable words seeking your hand.
This Dante writes a mystic rhapsody
Sometimes of you, sometimes of other loves.
He woos you in an idle dalliance,
But never asks in sweet solemnity
For leave to love and serve you all his days.
He is a man of words, that other of deeds.

61

You cannot spend long life of suns and storms
Beneath the vault of heaven, high over men,
Poised on an altar breathing heavy scents,
Invoked by music and adoring prayers,
You must be sheltered by a solid roof,
Fed, comforted, sustained by homely things.
Take love upon a glowing, happy hearth!

BEATRICE

I cannot, sir.

PORTINARI

Nay, Beatrice, you shall.
I have always cherished you, you could not know
How the world is, unsheltered and alone.

BEATRICE

Alone!

PORTINARI

My cup of life has brimmed with good,
Now, Justice beckons me to quit the feast.

BEATRICE

Speak not in riddles, father, for my ears
Hear only ringing terror. Are you ill?

PORTINARI

I had not thought to tell you, but, alas,
You crowd me to the leap. Beloved child,
A mortal sickness preys upon my frame.

BEATRICE

No, no!

PORTINARI

    There yet is time for deeds of love,
But I must see you safe before I die.
Simone is a wise and upright man,
He serves the state, he does not shrink and pine
And whistle tunes, but takes his sword in hand,
And drives the enemies of Florence forth;
Grieve not for me. I shall live long enough
To see you happy. Take Simone's hand.

BEATRICE

Some charlatan has told you ominous things,
For profit to himself.

PORTINARI

Go to the dance.

BEATRICE:

You are obeyed, sir. When we are alone
I must know everything about yourself
And why these fears and fancies come on you.

SIMONE

The music trips and pulses on the air
Like flitting feet alluring to the dance.
> [BEATRICE *gives him her hand. As she passes* DANTE, *she speaks to him aside.*

BEATRICE

You are the lover of Florence; therefore go
And battle for your lady in the lists,

64

The clarion blows, the lance is set in rest,
Deeds and not songs are needed.
                              [*She passes.*

DANTE

                    I will go.
Spirit of joy, whose light is blessedness,
Thou art the star that rules my destiny!
Upon the dark and troublous waves, where foam
Flutters from curling crests, thy silver thread
Trembling across yet guides along the deep.
Our souls are wed and I obey thy will.
Sweet smiling eyes, ye have redeemed my world!
I am made one with all warm, human things,
Not lonely now, not separate nor estranged,
For every tear that falls shall stain my cheek,
And every throb of passion shake my heart.
(*To* FORESE) Let us set out for camp.

FORESE
                    A miracle!

Act I	Dante and Beatrice

65

DANTE

I can sweep circles with the sword in air
Swift as a penstroke. And my feet are set
Upon a path where there is no returning.
Now use me for the trumpet of thy might,
Wind of the spirit—blown beneath the stars!

ACT II

SCENE I

Beside the Arno.

Enter from opposite sides DANTE *and* CAVALCANTI.

CAVALCANTI

All hail, my Dante, poet, conqueror,
Is it not enough to take Apollo's lyre,
But you must strip as well from Mars his sword?

DANTE

My plunder is a myth, my friend of friends!
How goes your Muse?

CAVALCANTI

She halts on tardy feet
Waiting to dance with thine.

DANTE

Is all well here?

CAVALCANTI
Fair Florence is beset;
A princess, girt with suitors cruel and base
That seek not love but gain.

DANTE
And you yourself?

CAVALCANTI
Corso Donati clamours for my life,
Dogging my footsteps with his hangers-on.
[*Men enter at back,* CORSO *with them.*

DANTE
Who are those men beyond?

CAVALCANTI
I know them not.
Let your sword rest! I heard at Campaldino
You led the van, shouting heroic words
That drew men after you to victory.

68

DANTE

I had much fear at first. The Aretines,
I mean the Ghibellines (some Aretines
Stood with us) but the men of Tuscany,
Routed the squadron of our cavaliers,
Pursuing them, parted their horse and foot,
Which we, united, one by one o'ercame.
Vieri de' Cerchi with me volunteered
Among the vanguard. Fleeing o'er the plain
I saw Buonconti, him of Montefeltro,
Pierced at the throat and bloodying the ground.
Let us not talk. There is a creeping throng,
A colony of rats from cellarways.

CAVALCANTI

Yea, they are Corso's men and there he lurks
Black in the shadow of the wall. And you
Are Guelf and must not fight against your own.
Then leave me.

DANTE
Guido, are you not my friend,

Yet think so slightly of me?   Man, stand back,
Or die on Dante's sword!
[They all engage.

CAVALCANTI

  We are overmatched.

DANTE

Not ten to one can overmatch me.

CAVALCANTI
       Fly,
And save yourself, sweet Dante!   I am done.
[He falls.

DANTE

Corso Donati!   Cease!   Draw off your men.
You shall not quit them; I will stop you, Dante,
Dante Alighieri!   You defile
Our cause!   You listen now.   Be not like wind
That fans and coaxes every smouldering gleam,

70

But quell contentious factions as soft rain
Stifles quick scattered sparks. Then peace will come
To bind fresh olives round our Lady's brow.

CORSO

[*To* DANTE] Poets enough are left, yet you shall live.

DANTE

I have not asked my life of you or any,
I say, you take a way to sure defeat
Of all things noble.

CORSO

[*To men*] Why do you hesitate?
Make way to Cavalcanti.

DANTE

Across me first!

CORSO

Fool, do you seek for death?

DANTE

                I shall not stir.
If death be seeking me, he will find me here!

CAVALCANTI

Nay, Dante, let me die, for you must live,
You are most precious—

DANTE

            Peace, my chief of friends!

CORSO

[*To* CAVALCANTI] Guido, I spare you for the nonce,
    slip off!
You poets have as many lives as cats!
And if we kill you, yet you live in rhyme!
But think not, Dante, that your eloquence
And lofty reasons moved me to this mercy—

Because Piccarda loved you, have your way.
Another time, Guido, another time!
[CAVALCANTI *goes*, FORESE *enters*.

FORESE

Dante, now welcome, comrade.

DANTE

      You as well
Weep at the sight of me! On Corso's cheeks
I saw salt drops make unaccustomed way!

FORESE

She is dead! Our little sister whom you loved!
Speak not of her—she is gone!

CORSO

      She was perverse,
In death even as in life—she pined at will
And died when she could serve us best—
        [*He goes.*

FORESE

Anon he rails at her and then he weeps!
Curses and broken words of tenderness
Mix on his lips, yet now, because she loved you
Spared his arch-enemy to save your life.

DANTE

Strangely love wills that life is born of death!
What is this death? We shrink and turn aside
At mention of his name; strive to escape,
And feel him touch our elbow; to forget,
And sudden we see the shade cross a loved face
Blighting its bloom.—Let me not think of death,
Lest he come with the thought.

FORESE
                     You fear to die.

DANTE

Hourly I fear lest Beatrice should die.
When a sweet maiden dies my heart is shaken,
Thinking how frail a casket holds my gem,

And visions come, a wailing in the night,
White and dishevelled women blown about,
Like torches wandering in the wind and rain.
There looms a shrouded presence by my bed
Upon whose dreadful brow is written, *Fate*,
And its face is in shadow.

FORESE

                       Didst thou hear
That noble Portinari is no more?

DANTE

I heard it yestereven as we rode in.
To-day my heart has watched with Beatrice,
Seeing her gracious countenance bowed low,
Wet with the tears of love, hearing her voice
That is so dulcet, broken with her sobs.

FORESE

Your fond imaginings have made you weep,
Take your hand from your eyes.

75

DANTE

                Her sorrow is mine.

FORESE

Then you were told of Portinari's death,
And no more news of Beatrice?

DANTE
                No more.
I go to seek her now. Here is a verse
I wrote of her good father.

FORESE
              Pause awhile.

DANTE

I must be gone. Above Fiesole
There hangs a purple cloud that pulses flame,
The low-browed hills are ominous, the earth
Has caught its breath, suspense impends and broods.
I am uneasy. Here the hoof-beats ring
Along the street beyond, each little noise
Appals the straining senses.

FORESE
             Go not yet.
                        [CECCO *enters*.

        CECCO
Ohè! I am in the heart of the labyrinth
And here is the roaring minotaur! I think
Some fool has dared to criticise your lays.
Poor Cavalcanti met I limping home,
And Baron Corso kicking at his men,
And here is Forese quaking in his shoes,
So every leg is quivering to your strains.
Last night beside his anvil the poor smith
Warbled your sonnets, smiting merrily.
You burst upon him, cast the hammer and tongs
Into the street and bent them—

           DANTE
                    Marring them,
Because he marred my implements, my songs,
He changed the words to suit his villain tunes.

77

CECCO

I applaud the valiant deed though not the cause—
What matter, so we fight and please ourselves!
Hit every head you see and soon there is sport,
The dullest clodpate smartly buffeted
Is valorous. Not the noblest battle hymn
Inspires to combat like a well-set blow.
If I were Pope I'd set the Church by the ears
And never rest till every Christian fought.

DANTE

Be silent, Cecco, impious buffoon!
Let be God's vicar. You profane sweet song
By ribald praising of a cobbler's girl,
Nothing is sacred—

CECCO

No, not even Dante!
Ah, Messer Ox, you jump though at the gadfly.
[*He goes.*

DANTE

Why should one strike at feathers with a sword!
Farewell, good friend, I hasten to my lady.

FORESE

Where would you go to seek her?

DANTE

                    At her home.

FORESE

Not at her father's house?

DANTE

              Why, there she dwells.

FORESE

You knew not she had wed dei Bardi?

DANTE

                     No.

FORESE

You will find her at his palace by the bridge.
But you will not go?

DANTE

     Yes. I shall go at once—
When I have rested on this bench a space.

FORESE

You grasp the stone as if you were grown blind.

DANTE

I think I have but now recovered sight.

FORESE

Your face is ghastly. Come away with me.
Red wine will put the courage in your blood.
There are many other maids as fair as she;
Time will outwear his charm, she will tire of him,
And then your chance—

DANTE

Take your hand from my sleeve.
Is that the house? I shall go seek her there.

FORESE

What can you have to say to Beatrice?
Best come away. There is thunder in the air,
Across the hills the wavering, steely rain
Falls like a curtain.

DANTE

I fear not the storm.

SCENE II

The hall in the house of SIMONE DEI BARDI.

BEATRICE *sits, surrounded by her nine maidens.*

SONG

O hush, for it is raining,
Slow drops the window staining
Like tears shed uncomplaining.

81

The birds are twittering sharply, none reposes,
    The messenger of love is here.
With parted crimson petals nod the roses;
The urn drips o'er with runnels crystal-clear;
    Spattering the gravel near:
The breeze sweet scent discloses,
Smell the fresh jessamine and heliotrope!
    Long lost and silent, long delays my lover,
        I hear in dreams his step draw nigher,
    The bliss, the lull of love, the garden cover,
        Echoes alone the strain of my desire.
        Yet far through frost or fire
    Song seeks the desert over
And heart finds heart beyond the wide world's scope.
The storm clouds coil and float like wraiths forsaken,
    The sobbing tempest catches breath;
Tell me, dear birds, if love shall ever waken
        Or if he slumbers in the drowse of death?
        Hark what the thunder saith!
Soft rain like dew is shaken;
Spring bringeth love in tears but brings not hope.

BEATRICE

The thunder rolls along between the hills.
Was that a step that sounded through the rain;
And now a knocking at the outer door?
Run, Adonella, call the porter. Run!

FIRST MAIDEN

Madonna, the white lightning on the draught!

BEATRICE

Stay, little coward. Hark, one knocks like fate.
Almost it shakes my heart. Lucia, go!
      [*Second maiden goes.*
Some one is coming with great need to come,
Or quick desire to follow in rain and flame,
The thunder bellowing after.
     [*Second maiden returns.*
     Who is there?

SECOND MAIDEN

Madonna, it is Messer Dante, wet
And thinner in his damp cloak than a lath.
       [DANTE *enters.*

Act II   Dante and Beatrice

BEATRICE
Sir, you are chill, drenched by the driving storm.
Bring him some wine, spiced wine.

DANTE
                              I thank you, no.
My cloak is thick.

BEATRICE
Call Messer Simone.

DANTE
Madonna,-

BEATRICE
Stay, not yet, you need not call.

DANTE
My errand is with you.

BEATRICE
Go then, my girls.
                    [*Maidens go out.*

It is many months since I have seen your face,
But tidings of your valour came to us.
I see you shivering.   Take the wine.

DANTE

        I drink
Of Lethe, the one wine that quenches thirst.
Surely they brew such liquor here, Madonna
And you have quaffed wine of oblivion.
This is not Lethe and I cannot find it.
Where do you keep it, in what cellarage?
Beseech you, send, that I may drink with you.

BEATRICE

What would you forget, Dante?

DANTE

       The past,
But most of all my songs.

BEATRICE

       Then I must drink;
Deeply indeed, ere I forget your songs.

DANTE
You gave me poison!

BEATRICE
Sir!

DANTE
              Be not afraid;
I speak in symbols, merely words and signs
Of souls, not bodies; not of earthly death,—
Poison not to my body, but my soul.
The pearl I gave you, perfect, exquisite,
Pure as the moon, with shadowy rose and gold,
You have dissolved within an acrid draught.
Here is the song I made you yesterday.
Then was the golden sun my friend in heaven.
I was a part of spring among the flowers
That trembled in the grass; borne on the breeze,
A wreath of cloud, over dim violet sky.
I know not the grey world I wander in
Here, through this vacant day.
                    [*He gives her the poem.*

BEATRICE

[*Reads.*] Was all my sorrow and loss so close to you
Dear and great poet, that you wept with me?
How shall words thank you for this gift of gifts?

DANTE

Hark to the rain's innumerable lips
That whisper of soft mysteries. And now
The tremour hushes while the thunder calls.
Your voice shall be the voice of the falling rain
And mine the thunder. Beatrice, Beatrice!
How dark it grows. Now for a flash you stand
Radiant in white fire. Yet you are gone.
The woman I have sought and followed and found
Was never here on earth. She wore your form
And smiled your sacred smile; looked from your eyes,
Whence Love enshrined pierces the hearts of men.

BEATRICE

I do not understand you.

DANTE

              Listen awhile.
When I went forth because you bade me go
To combat for my country, you forsook me.
I cannot even say the word—that word.
You left me. You have given your beauteous flesh—

BEATRICE

I cannot hear this. You are distracted, sir.

DANTE

You shall not leave me yet. If ever one thought
Of kindness or of mercy turned toward me,
If all my songs kindled a flickering spark
Of pity or of wonder, if my poor life
Has merit in your eyes, if there is worth
In me as man, such as the unlettered hind
Tending his flock might know; then hear me now.

BEATRICE

In all life's usage you have been supreme.
Shall I not hear you in humility?

DANTE
Look not so innocently, for you knew.
Forgive me, Bice, if you did not know,
Now, though I never speak on earth again,
Though I be spurned, I shall fulfill my song.
The love that companied you shall waken you,
And he shall feed you on my flaming heart.

BEATRICE
Dante, almost I fear you.

DANTE
              That is well.
These singers that like sparrows in the rain
Chirp amorous ditties, quick from spray to spray,
These are not like the nightingale, whose cry
Eternal, is his pain for one lost love.
Have you forgot the festival of May?
To my child-eyes you were a miracle,
The youngest of the angels, your slight form
Robed in clear crimson, and your face, a pearl,—
Have you forgot that day in tender spring,
The boy, your playfellow?

Act II   Dante and Beatrice

BEATRICE
Was it yourself?
Have you remembered even a crimson frock?

DANTE
I saw you and the spirit of my life,
Deep dwelling, hid within my secret heart,
Trembled and knew the presence of its God.
Often I stole away to gaze on you
When you knew nothing, and exultingly
Forever with me bore the vision of you
Limned on my spirit, and no other face
Has made me turn one wandering glance aside.
The air I breathed was sweet with thoughts of you
Sleep overtook me conning every charm
Softly unto myself; you were my dreams,
My lips before I woke murmured your name.
I loved you as no woman yet was loved.
I should have been all yours, eternally,
Grown glorious and great in the sight of you
As great trees wax beneath a tropic sun.
Now I shall pine and wither as in long drouth

When shrivelling branches shed their sallow leaves
Stunted and desolate. Thief, thief of life,
You have reft away my spirit's dignities,
The crown of wisdom, mantle of my peace,
Chalice of faith and sceptre of restraint.
I am dethroned, I shall seek hovels now;
A doting madman, cheat myself with beads,
Refuse and straws, calling them gems and gold.
I shall love many women with little love
And fire and frost alternate in my blood:
Fall in strange passions and hot ecstasies
Pursue lost music in the earth and air.

BEATRICE

If you loved righteousness you would be righteous
And only thus. Not of a woman's love
Is born the solemn virtue, hope of the world.

DANTE

You cheated me, bright wonder of the flesh
That I have worshipped; I was nothing—only

A pitiful creature, mocked and played upon
And cast aside.

BEATRICE
    You were my master poet,
Great and imperishable and girt with visions,
When I drew near, your immortality
Flamed round me till my senses dazzled—

DANTE
          God,
This is the truth!   You love me, Beatrice.

BEATRICE
Hush, for one breathing instant, for the wind
Has sunk, and the rain ceased and the air is still—
The light and crying are gone from the pale sky.

DANTE
I hear the birds, each fluting to his love,
That sweetly answers—there is a nightingale
High in the cypress!   There is another flying.
Now, he will answer far away.   You hear?

BEATRICE

There is a voice as well.

DANTE

It is Casella—

BEATRICE

Pacing the pergola.

DANTE

He soothes the storm
With magic sounds.

BEATRICE

I think it is your song.

CASELLA

[*Without*] *'Mid mystic measures intricate and sweet*
My dazed thought a perilous passage takes,
Rapt into rare and unaccustomed ways.
Alas, my stricken sense no strength essays
To attain and lay my worship at her feet!

Act II   Dante and Beatrice

DANTE
I have lost it now.

BEATRICE
Hush, he will turn and then—

CASELLA
Let censure fall alone on my oblation,
Whose rhymes reach not my lady's high degree,
For mind is sunk in spirit's adoration,
And speech may never with such influence move,
As shall command the harmonies of love.

BEATRICE
Do you remember on that long-dead evening
Casella ended and your voice began
Remeasuring music, and my father came.
Next day I learned the song—but you had gone.

DANTE
My roaming songs, that fled my wintry days,
Have rested in your heart, sweet lady of spring.
And has my speech found favour? My heavier words?

BEATRICE
You spoke the thoughts toward which my spirit strove,
Nay, even the motions of my hidden heart.

DANTE
I was all yours that am forever yours,
It matters not to pause and ponder thereof,
We are together. Time is not for us,
We are eternal and love eternally.

BEATRICE
How dark it grows.

DANTE
     The storm returns amain
Heavy in purple. A chattering of the leaves
Shakes all the treetops and a throbbing light
Quickens and goes. I cannot see your face,
But your slight form blots on the window's glare
With every flash. The perfume of your dress
Stifles me here. Hark to the warring winds
That beat against the darkness on and on.

BEATRICE
Throw open a lattice: let me feel the air!

DANTE
The night is warm: how fresh the garden smells.
The flowers can teach us all that we should know,
Whose perfume is the exquisite call of love.
Will you not tell me why you left me?

BEATRICE
No.
Had you been here, perhaps it had not been.

DANTE
Where was this body was a faithful heart
Quickening for you.

BEATRICE
Yet you had said no word;
No prayer of man to woman; only songs,
Visions and prophecies and ecstasies.

DANTE

I will say *I love you* till the constant cry
Outwear the iteration of the birds.

BEATRICE

It is too late.   The door is shut to joy.
I doubted everything when you were gone,
Myself and you and love.   Why did you go?
Distance does sorry things to human hearts.
And do you know that like a wave of the sea
Is every passion in man?   Joy, love and grief
Rise up and swell and break and then withdraw.
Now you must go.

DANTE

    Shall I turn to the storm
And pray the lightning to seek out my heart?
Listen, my Beatrice: the spinning Fates
Wove close the patterns of your life and mine,
They blend and knit harmonious thread to thread
By strong, immortal fingers intertwined,
Nor can we ravel a warp of destiny.

Act II   Dante and Beatrice

97

BEATRICE

No more, sweet Dante.

DANTE

     Listen to the rain:
It whispers with soft lips and thunder calls
And levin writes in fire the word of truth —
Love hath united us past peradventure.
Out there across the border only last year
Paolo and Francesca in Rimini
Died—but died happy. We have not lived at all.
Now let us live, and if needs be find death
In some sweet way together. Come with me.

BEATRICE

Bring in the lights!
  [*Maidens enter with lights and circle round
   her, place them in sconces and withdraw.*
     There is no more to say,
Seeing you have said your last worst word of me.
You cannot raise your lids to see my face.

DANTE
I would honour you forever.

BEATRICE
            Lift up your chin.
Do you think thus of me?   So swiftly false?
Unfaithfulness is in the deeps of hell
And treachery to those that love us, worst
Of the dark crimes peopling the chill abyss.
What of that man, my honourable spouse?
Am I not one with him in the sight of God,
Made so by Holy Church and both our wills?

DANTE
But if you love me?

BEATRICE
            Shall I open a door
To let foul beasts among our household gods?
You must go from me, sir, I do not trust you.

DANTE
Bice, forgive me.

BEATRICE
Do you weep for that.
You shall weep bitterer tears for other sword.
You have slain him through whom all mankind
    towered.
Who is this creature that will leave my love
To run with harlots? Who will even come
To purpose mischief to the woman he loves,
Luring her toward the darkness? In my love
Hast thou not said thou followed holiness,
Growing toward heaven, companioned by the stars?
Wilt thou forsake me now to give thyself
Unto foul things that canker and defile
God's image? Didst thou mean by thy wild words
That since thou couldst not have thy joy fulfilled
Thou wouldst forsake all good and turn thy face
To follow evil, to pursue false visions
That never pay their promise? Answer me.
Dante, thou must confess it.

DANTE
Yea.

100

BEATRICE
                        Alas,
Let me not see again that face of yours
Which I have bowed before with reverence,
And while I live let me not hear the name
I coupled with the names of saints and heroes.
Now art thou dead; for this is death eternal:
Not the mere passing of the mortal breath
To be with God and leave within our hearts
Immortal memories, but corrupt death,
The soul and not the body turned to clay.
Still droops thy head. Look now upon mine eyes;
They shall condemn thee.

DANTE
               Mercy, Beatrice!
                                   [He faints.

BEATRICE
O, dearest head, may I not even lift thee?
Not cherish thee, fevered and beaten child?

DANTE
Above the flood! Hold me above the flood.

Act II   Dante and Beatrice

101

BEATRICE

Be comforted: I hold thee, thou wilt not sink.

DANTE

Who are thou, spirit?

BEATRICE

Even Beatrice.

DANTE

Alas, my life returns in agony.
My cheek is wet with tears that are not mine.

BEATRICE

Thou art born again of water and of the spirit.

DANTE

May God be thanked, who hath restored my soul,
And hath forgiven me as thou forgivest.
Yet still a voice within me will not cease.
Deeply I sinned when my flesh spoke to thee,
But my soul did not sin that called thee mine.
These are laws written on our hearts, above

The laws that man hath made. Not ever again
Shall I offend thee, even in my hid thoughts;
Fear not, my love, there is no earth therein.

BEATRICE

Even as thou offerest I accept thy gift.
There shall be quiet places in our lives
Wherein the pilgrim spirit, journeying, finds
Pathways of peace and of humility.
And there this love of ours shall be a light
Guiding us to that river whose limpid streams
Gently shall wash away our stains and tears,
Assuaging then at last our bitter thirst.

DANTE

My poignant loneliness, like subtle flame
Patiently borne, shall purify the dross.
Dost thou weep, Beatrice?

BEATRICE

                Leave me not yet,
I am not strong. How shall I fill the days,

Vacant, intolerable, until I die?
We have lost everything; nothing is left.

DANTE

Courage is left, gallantly hour by hour
To serve man and to save; the vivid earth
Thrilling with song is left; the solemn hills,
The restless flashing sea of fluctuant waves,
The silver hosts of the assembled stars.

BEATRICE

My poet, thou shalt never be bereft,
Faring with genius and with liberty;
But canst thou teach a woman how to live?

DANTE

Be thine all-beautiful and blessed self.
Thy holy eyes are sun-smit emeralds!
Delight of God, benignant grace is thine,
None can end ill that once hath spoken with thee.
All things shall wear away. My bitter life
Finally shall be as it had not been,

Save that the echo of its singing love
Shall dwell in music on the winds of time,
And of the priceless gift of thy great soul
Nothing be lost that may enrich mankind.
Thy voice shall summon and thy spirit speak
Through my lips, one with me eternally.

BEATRICE

May God be very near to thee, my Dante.

DANTE

He shall be ever nearer while I live.
I shall ascend to meet thee, Beatrice,
Through darkness climbing up to greet the dawn.
Now must I part from you.   Before I go
May I not kiss you?

BEATRICE

Never, while I live.

DANTE

Forgive me.   Will you say *I love you?*

BEATRICE
                    No.

DANTE
I must die starving then.   You are so young,
In many years to live in many deeds,
Shall this one hour be lost and be forgot?

BEATRICE
I promise, as you have given unto me
The supreme gift, one last least recompense.
I must be silent.   Impermissible,
Now, were that word, but ere you come to die
You shall receive my answer.   Rest in this.

DANTE
Shall I be satisfied?

BEATRICE
          Only have faith.   [*He goes.*
My heart is torn away out of my breast.
Dante, return! Love—!
                         [SIMONE *enters.*

SIMONE
Did you call?

BEATRICE
No, no!
Leave me a little, I beseech you, sir.

SIMONE
Alas, sweet Beatrice, your hand is cold!

BEATRICE
Soon I will come to you. [*He goes.*] Thou seest, God,
My shame; this horror, love's sanctuary defiled:
He holds my body that holds not my heart,
And he to whom my thought incessantly
Turns, like a plant whose tender leaves seek light,
Shall never come to illuminate the hours
That other wastes in darkness; drudging hours
Of infelicity, that might have been
Momently glorious, each a blessed thing.
Father, I know to-day you weep in heaven.

You built my dungeon with a careful hand,
I should have followed Dante through this world
Barefoot and happy. I am caught in toils,
A mastered creature, fettered, stifled, held!
Rescue me, death, from days that are accursed,
Wash with thy waters from my mind and heart
Remembrances of things that are a stain.
Deliver me, kind messenger of God,
And fetch me to my Lover amid the stars.

ACT III

SCENE I

Dante's *lodgings. He is pacing up and down, pausing to write.* Forese *enters.*

FORESE

No words for me?

DANTE

          No words from thee, I pray.
Dost thou not see I write? Beseech thee, go!
Stay not a breath of time. Thou breakest the thread
That held my winged thought earth's prisoner.
The filament is snapped, the bird is gone!
Stay if thou wilt or go, sing, laugh or wail,
Patter thy tedious talk of common things,
Turn out my larder, gorge thy ravenous maw,—

Act III   Dante and Beatrice

I saw thee sniff my pastry long ago.
Live out thy life or die within this room,
Thou hast done all thy damnable worst on me!

    FORESE
     [Calling from the window.
His black scrip is unpacked and thrown about
My ears, there cannot be a single curse
Or malediction left to fling at you.
  [Several friends enter, among them CINO,
   CECCO *and* CASELLA.

    CINO
Most gentle Dante—

    FORESE
  There is none gentle here!

    CINO
Dear poet, read us what you wrote but now.
It was of her to whom your exquisite song
Rings ever clearer, ravishing our ears,
A lark that quivers up to praise the morn.

DANTE

Cino, thou hast a heart, not a dry leaf
Like that Forese. I will read to thee.
The joy of June, the plenitude of life
Is poured from the blue sun-searched firmament,
Where the majestic clouds like domes of snow
Pass imperceptibly. The swallows' cry
Dispelled my dreams before the silver dawn,
I rose and breathed the warm and perfumed wind,
And, like a prayer, my song went up to God.
I am a thing of earth and earthly days,
Born of the sin and travail of the race,
Wrought of its dust and tears and bitter blood,
She is not so, my comforter and my guide,
A visitant from heavenly shores, the light
Of distant stars within her eyes, the smile
Of angels on her lips. My only worth
Has been my love. I may not think of her
Without a passion of exceeding praise.
Today I quaffed a wine of happiness,
And numbering the gifts of God's good will,
In that His Beatrice has gazed on me,

Act III   Dante and Beatrice

III

By her dear virtue had begun this song:—
So long and long hath love my life possessed,
  So wonted is become his mastery,
    That even as once he seemed unkind to me,
Now blissfully he reigns within my breast.
Thus when his ministers my courage wrest
    Till tremulous the vital spirits flee,
    My face is blanched with the swift ecstacy
Of utter sweetness on my senses pressed.
Love gathering over me supreme control,
    Teaches my grievous sighs to utter speech,
        My lady to beseech,
To grant again the grace that lifts my soul.
    Thus it befalls when I her face behold,
    Whose fair humility no words have told.
            [*While he reads* CAVALCANTI *enters, saying with his lips " Beatrice is dead." As* DANTE *ends he looks up.*

DANTE

And here, like fierce March wind that slays the flowers,
Forese burst upon me, rent and tossed

The fragile petals of my blossoming song,
Which I bewailed. Why do you gaze on me
With those blank eyes? Who entered while I read?
Guido! What news?
     [*All rise and move toward the door.*
      Canst thou not answer me?
Is Florence threatened?

CAVALCANTI
    No. No public grief,
But loss to thee, poor D nte.

DANTE
      Loss to me?
What have I God or man could take from me?
There is nothing mine precious in the eyes of men.
Only the rich tremble to hear ill news,
Only the happy are fearful. I have naught,
Except the glorious lady of my mind.
Except my Beatrice. Not Beatrice!
She is not—No, God would not rob the world
That needs her so. Guido, she is not dead?

Act III   Dante and Beatrice

113

CAVALCANTI
Alas, she is dead.

DANTE
"How dost thou sit alone
O, city who wert so full of people,—how
Is she become a widow who was great
Among the nations!"

CAVALCANTI
Idly, day by day,
Dame Fortune turns her wheel, and who was high
Serene and radiant, lies low in earth.

DANTE
Sorrow has entered to abide with me
And hand in hand Rancour and Pain draw near,
And Love comes habited in weeds of black
Stumbling, tear-blinded.

CINO
Thou, whom God made wise,
Dispel the cloud of death from face and heart;

Since in this dolorous world, dazed and distressed,
We are haled onward, thou shouldst now rejoice
That she is safe with God and prays for thee.

DANTE

She is not dead. I saw her two days since,
Perhaps a little pale. She is ever pale,
She has but swooned. Guido, it is not—?

CAVALCANTI
                Yes.
Dear Dante,—

DANTE
                Leave me! If I think with you
The soul is shrivelled in a fiery tomb.
Forese, speak! God lives, Beatrice lives.

FORESE

My friend, I fear that Beatrice is dead.

DANTE

Where art thou gone, O sovereign intellect?

115

CECCO

This death is a dullard! If I were but death,
I would look my father up that hugs his gold
So tight the florins squeak. Let me go out!
                                    [*He goes.*

DANTE

Shall I live through my life, day after day,
Minute by minute, and not see her face?
It is not possible. Why, I remember
How soft her lips curled when she smiled at me.
Shall I forget her slow smile's miracle?
I shall watch enviously all who die;
See the door clang behind them, fancy a light
Whereto they enter, leaving me in cold.
What can you say to me, Forese?

FORESE
                         Nothing.
I know the Church could tell you many things;
I am not wise, I have forgot them all.
Send for a priest. I never saw, myself,
One that had died and lived again.

DANTE

                      Get hence!
Guido, where is my lady and my love?

CAVALCANTI

Her immortality is in our hearts.

DANTE

Ring true, pure gold of friendship! Let them dream,
These folk that cringe before an unknown god,
The deaf, dumb, blind creation of their hearts,
The prop they have made to hold their feebleness,
The shadow cast by their soul's fervid light,
The image that they follow through the sand,—
Domed temples, golden over the brown walls,
Spires of celestial amber shimmering,
City of many mansions, each a home—

FORESE

He is mad! Dear Dante, this is blasphemy;
Vengeance will fall from God.

DANTE
                What will He do,
Having wrought out His worst forever on me?
I bore the agony of my baulked love,
I set my flame upon His altar, prayed,
Fasted, grew holy; I took my heavy sorrow
As from His hand; and now, what has He done?
Am I not dead? Tell me, when shall I die?
Let it be soon if any of you have hearts.
Give me escape from the endless, bitter world.

CAVALCANTI
Dante, this is not worthy, no, nor brave.
Thy spirit should transcend the fury of chance
And cruelty of death; so shouldst thou grow
Strong through thy pain, sweet through remembered love.

DANTE
This love that is our agony and bliss
Is an illusion. I will avoid the heights
And lay me in low meadows, weave my crown
Of thornless blooms.

CAVALCANTI
Desire shall gnaw your heart.

DANTE
My heart is stone: I shall not feel again.

CAVALCANTI
[*To* CASELLA] Cleave his hard heart with the swift sword of song.

CASELLA
[*Sings*] *Love in my mind a mighty music wakes*
And yearning unto him my voice I raise
Impassioned to declare my lady's praise.

DANTE
Cease, cease!

FORESE
Casella, he will die in tears.

CAVALCANTI
I bade him sing: no man shall question it.

CASELLA

'Mid mystic measures intricate and sweet
  My dazed thought a perilous passage takes
  Rapt into rare and unaccustomed ways.
  Alas, my stricken sense no strength essays
To attain and lay my worship at her feet.
For who shall soar on seraph pinion fleet
  Weighted with clogs of dull humanity?
Through mortal lips the vision of blessed eyes
  Seek to immortalize—
  A beauty unbeheld of all that see?

DANTE

My will is quiet, my spirit is appeased.

CAVALCANTI

Vanquish him, ere he fail of truth and honour.

CASELLA

Let censure fall alone on my oblation,
  Whose rhymes reach not my lady's high degree.
For mind is lost in spirit's adoration,

*And speech may never with such influence move
As shall command the harmonies of love.*

      DANTE
I am broken beneath the harrow. Leave me now.
For I believe that love shall seek for me
Through all the distant ways from farthest heaven.
           [*They go out.*
Where are my tablets? Let me draw a face,
An angel's face, with lineaments like hers.
Angels flame-winged about her; she most fair.
She strays in glory inaccessible
To our desirous fancy's utmost flight,
       [GEMMA *enters, unperceived.*
Removed from sullen earth, cloud-hung with care,
Removed perhaps from pain-filled thoughts of us.
Hast thou forgot me in beatitude,
Bright Beatrice, and thou, sweet, fond Piccarda?
        [*He perceives* GEMMA.
When didst thou enter?

      GEMMA
   May I—may I—come?

DANTE

What wouldst thou have?   Trembling and pale, my
 child?

GEMMA

I sent the word that Beatrice was dead
By Cavalcanti, for he loves you best.
I would not enter while they talked so loud,
Those rough, unknowing men, but when they went
Thoughts of your loneliness constrained my feet.

DANTE

Why dost thou weep?

GEMMA

Dante, I mourn with thee.

DANTE

Speak not so pitiful lest my heart break.

GEMMA

Love sends me to thee that thy soul find rest.

DANTE
Gentle and pensive face compassionate,
Thou drawest mine eyes to thee—

GEMMA
                           Thy wasted eyes
Red-circled as with crown of martyrdom.

DANTE
I thank thee for thy pity. Pray thee, go,
For tears are rising from my heart and yet
I cannot weep before thee.

GEMMA
              I will go,
And may a kindly thought of me abide
Whispering, "Thou art not alone, one lives
Who waits, in sorrow for thy misery." [*Goes.*

DANTE
What spirit is this that comes to comfort me,
Speaking the speech of love? O doubtful breast,
Now art thou severed with opposing hosts,

The soul and heart at war. Shall I escape
From so much bitterness and be at peace?
For my beloved is gone, a torch outblown,
A vanished star that leaves my heaven obscure;
Silence encompasses the ended song.
I am forgotten. If any word or sign
Could reach across the void to summon me
I should not faint perhaps. O vacant night—
Only the gloom to straining ears and eyes!
She promised me that ere I came to die
I should receive her answer, know at last
The heart of her and be therewith content.
She has forgotten as He whom once I served
Forgot Piccarda's prayer that my worst need
Be comforted. I am forsaken of all.
        [SIMONE *enters*.
    SIMONE
Is Messer Dante here within?

    DANTE
     Not you!
Of all men in this city why have you come?
Go from me, for I know not what I do.

SIMONE

Talk if you will; wild talking is your trade.

DANTE

You come to gloat over my emptiness
Who all your days were rich and gratified.

SIMONE

Now you grow dull; you know I am bereft.

DANTE

You taunt me with your happy memories.
I have been choked, beaten, trodden in the dust,
Denied the fragments scattered to the dogs,
Not even crumbs—not even crumbs. O God,
Thy burning scorn intolerable, has seared
My outworn heart!

SIMONE

          You need not cry so loud;
God hears you not and I hear easily.

Act III   Dante and Beatrice

DANTE
You have been glutted with the wine of the gods.

SIMONE
Dante, my wife is dead.

DANTE
    Say not that word!

SIMONE
Shall I not name her? Beatrice is dead.

DANTE
You had a wife! Have I had anything—
Anything here but agony? She is dead
And you are young and she is gone from you;
You thought you loved her—

SIMONE
      Silence, raving fool!

DANTE

I am patient of your wrath.   You thought you loved
    her.
I know that it is so.   Why are you here?
Of all the beings peopling the wide earth
We two should not have met upon this day.

SIMONE

She sent me, Dante.

DANTE

                Sent—but she is dead.
She thought of me before she died?   O speak!
You will tell me what she said?   Forgive me, sir,
You will not be so cruel to punish me
By silence for my words?   You will tell me?

SIMONE
                                                Yes.
Hush, Messer Dante.   You are naught to me,
And what you say is naught.   I will do her bidding.
She did not suffer long—

DANTE
    Suffered!

SIMONE
                  Not long.
No remedy was lacking, love and gold
Squandered their strength—

DANTE
        You could not give her joy.

SIMONE
You are too contemptible to tread upon!
Can you not hold your peace until I end?

DANTE
Nature, not this thy blame, no silver frost
Nor quivering heat drove this sweet spirit forth
From thy domain; she was too fair a thing
To dwell amid the noisome haunts of men,
Unworthy neighbours to such blessedness.

SIMONE

When she perceived that her last hour drew on
She bade me promise that I would come to you,
When she had died, and bring you unto her
And let you kiss her once upon the lips.

DANTE

My God, forgive me, for her gentle sake
Who loved me when she died—Thy Beatrice!
Let me go to her where she sleeps in peace.
[*To* SIMONE] There are no words can thank you.

SIMONE

       Then attempt none.
I have fulfilled my promise; let us go.

DANTE

Pass on before and I will follow you.
         [SIMONE *goes.*
I am not fit, O God, to come to her,
But thou shalt lead my pilgrim steps at last

Through many shadows to the eternal dawn,
Where she beholds Thy presence evermore.
A distant music trembles on the air
While deeper choruses and hymning choirs
Answer in diapason pure as light,
And children's thrilling voices carolling
A silver descant echo over heaven.
The angels cry *Hosannah!* and blow loud
Their fiery trumpets, and a radiance beams
Like summer sunrise on a dappled sky.
Behold a golden rose with spreading leaves,
Ring above ring, the concourse of the saints,
Exhaling praise like fervid perfume! There
Is Beatrice, bright in immortal youth,
Robed in clear crimson, glory in her eyes.
I shall not turn from thee, O blessed face
That drew me forth, a slave, to liberty,
But God shall grant me grace that my poor life
Persever till I speak in thy dear praise
Such things as never yet were said of woman,
Then may my soul have leave to come to thee.
I see thee smile in welcome. Round thy brow

130

The splendour from on high reflected weaves
An aureole: thy prayers ascend for me,
And my desire and will united seek
That love that moves the sun and all the stars.

By SARA KING WILEY

The Coming of Philibert   Cloth, 12mo, $1.25 *net*

"A poetic drama of dignity and charm . . . treated with delicacy of fancy and dramatic strength, containing passages full of sheer poetic beauty, and situations full of action and force."—*The Book News Monthly.*

Alcestis, and Other Poems   Cloth, 16mo, $0.75 *net*

"The 'Alcestis' is carefully built on a Greek model. There is something Greek, too, in the cheerful love of man and of life and in the marble purity of the form of the poem. The lament of Admetus after the death, the sudden sense of emptiness and void is very finely done, for Mrs. Drummond (Sara King Wiley) has an almost Keatsian power over the fine and memory-haunting phrase. This volume is the most exquisite blossom of a delicately nurtured womanhood and a high and effective culture."— LOUISE COLLIER WILLCOX in the *North American Review.*

Poems, Lyrical and Dramatic

Cromwell. A Play   Cloth, 12mo, $1.50 *net*

Mr. MABIE said of these in the *Outlook:* "They give evidence of a true gift, so clearly do they reveal the writer's sensitiveness to poetic meanings and the delicate skill with which her faculty responds to her insight."

PUBLISHED BY
THE MACMILLAN COMPANY
64–66 FIFTH AVENUE, NEW YORK

A LIST OF PLAYS

By WINSTON CHURCHILL
The Title-Mart   75 cents *net*
A comedy of American Society, wherein love and the young folks go their way in spite of their elders and ambition.

By CLYDE FITCH
The Climbers   75 cents *net*
The Girl with the Green Eyes   75 cents *net*
Her Own Way   75 cents *net*
The Stubbornness of Geraldine   75 cents *net*
The Truth   75 cents *net*
Ingenious satires on modern society, unhackneyed in incident, piquant in humor, showing minute observation happily used. Each is bound in cloth, with white paper label.

By THOMAS HARDY
The Dynasts: A Drama of the Napoleonic Wars. *In Three Parts.* Each $1.50 *net*

By LAURENCE HOUSMAN
Bethlehem: A Musical Nativity Play $1.25 *net*

By HENRY ARTHUR JONES
Mrs. Dane's Defence   75 cents *net*
Michael and His Lost Angel   75 cents *net*
Rebellious Susan   75 cents *net*
Saints and Sinners   75 cents *net*

PUBLISHED BY
THE MACMILLAN COMPANY
64–66 FIFTH AVENUE, NEW YORK

BY HENRY ARTHUR JONES (*Continued*)
   The Crusaders   75 cents *net*
   The Infidel   75 cents *net*
   The Tempter   75 cents *net*
   The Whitewashing of Julia   75 cents *net*
      Each of these well-known plays is bound in cloth, with white paper label.

BY JACK LONDON
   Scorn of Women   Cloth, $1.25 *net*
      The scenes are laid in the far north, Mr. London's special province.

BY PERCY MACKAYE
   The Canterbury Pilgrims $1.25 *net*
   Fenris the Wolf. A Tragedy $1.25 *net*
   Jeanne d'Arc $1.25 *net*
   The Scarecrow $1.25 *net*
   Mater $1.25 *net*
   Sappho and Phaon $1.25 *net*

BY WILLIAM VAUGHN MOODY
   The Great Divide   *Now Ready*

BY STEPHEN PHILLIPS
   Nero $1.25 *net*
   Ulysses $1.25 *net*
   The Sin of David $1.25 *net*

BY STEPHEN PHILLIPS and J. COMYNS CARR
   Faust   —————— $1.25 *net*

PUBLISHED BY
THE MACMILLAN COMPANY
64–66 FIFTH AVENUE, NEW YORK

BY ARTHUR UPSON
    The City (a drama), and Other Poems $1.25 *net*

BY SARA KING WILEY
    Alcestis (a play) and Other Poems $0.75 *net*
    The Coming of Philibert $1.25 *net*

MR. WILLIAM WINTER'S *Version of*
    Mary of Magdala $1.25 *net*
        An adaptation from the original of Paul Heyse; used by Mrs. Fiske.

BY WILLIAM BUTLER YEATS
    Where there is Nothing   Cloth, $1.25 *net*
        Limited large paper edition, $5.00 *net*
    The Hour Glass, and Other Plays $1.25 *net*
    In the Seven Woods $1.00 *net*
        NOTE.—Volume II. of the Collected Edition of Mr. Yeats's Poetical Works includes five of his dramas in verse: "The Countess Cathleen," "The Land of Heart's Desire," "The King's Threshold," "On Baile's Strand," and "The Shadowy Waters."   Cloth, $1.75 *net*

BY WILLIAM BUTLER YEATS and LADY GREGORY
    The Unicorn from the Stars and Other Plays $1.50 *net*
        Attractively bound in decorated cloth.

BY ISRAEL ZANGWILL
        Author of "Children of the Ghetto," etc.
    The Melting-Pot $1.25 *net*

PUBLISHED BY
THE MACMILLAN COMPANY
64–66 FIFTH AVENUE, NEW YORK